Thank You, Prague!

A Guide and a Memoir

By Jaroslav B. and Sara D. Tusek

Sara D. Tusek, Executive Editor

International Leadership Institute Publications

PO Box 950-788, Lake Mary, FL 32795-0788

USA

www.ili.cc

Publication History:

First edition, 2026

ISBN: 979-8-9957256-0-2

Cover and text design: Noah Shepherd, NY, NY

Cover photo: Image by Bronisław Dróżka

Published by International Leadership Institute Publications:

The Professor's Book of Readings. Sara Tusek, editor. International Leadership Institute Publications, Lake Mary, FL, 2022.

Read and Write Like a Professor. Sara Tusek. International Leadership Institute Publications, Lake Mary, FL, 2020.

Reinventing Your Future. Jaroslav B. Tusek and Sara Tusek. International Leadership Institute Publications, Lake Mary, FL, 2019.

Leaders to Follow. Jaroslav B. Tusek with Sara Tusek. International Leadership Institute Publications, Lake Mary, FL, 2018.

Prague for Beginners: Finding Myself in Prague. Sara Tusek. International Leadership Institute Publications, Lake Mary, FL, 2017.

21st Century Jobs. Jaroslav B. Tusek and Sara Tusek. International Leadership Institute Publications, Lake Mary, FL, 2009.

From Idea to Book in Five Steps. Sara Tusek. International Leadership Institute Publications, Lake Mary, FL, 2019.

Three Things You Can't Do in Prague. Jaroslav B. Tusek and Sara Tusek. Servant Leaders Press, Ponte Vedra Beach, FL, 2006.

Your Career Passport. Jaroslav B. Tusek and Sara D. Shepherd (Tusek). International Leadership Institute Publications, Ponte Vedra Beach, FL, 2nd Edition, 1993; 1st Edition, 1991.

Leaders to Follow, 1991-2012; *Business Briefs,* 1992-1997. *Careers*, 1987-2012; *Servant Leaders*, 2005-2012; *continuous conversion*, 2006-2012 *ALOE: A Lesson on English*, 2007-2012.

Other publications:

East Tennessee Business Journal/Chattanooga Business Journal. Jaroslav B. and Sara Tusek, contributing editors and columnists, 1993-2008.

College to First Job: Step by Step. Sara D. Shepherd (Tusek). The University of the South, Sewanee, TN, 1988.

Looking Ahead. Sara D. Shepherd (Tusek). The University of the South, Sewanee, TN, 1988.

Career Development Handbook. Sara D. Shepherd (Tusek). The University of the South, Sewanee, TN, 1987.

Designing Your Future. Jaroslav B. Tusek. St. Lawrence University, Canton, NY, 1985.

Career Development Kit for Future Leaders: An Introduction to Career Management. Jaroslav B. Tusek. American Management Association, Hamilton, NY, 1984.

Career Search Kit for International Students: A Handbook of Sources for the International Job Market. Jaroslav B. Tusek. New York Institute of Technology, New York, NY, 1983.

THANK YOU, PRAGUE!

We invite you to visit the amazing city of Prague with us. Imagine this little book as your personal guide to Prague, written by Prague-born Jaroslav (Jarda) and his wife, American-born Sara.

I [Jarda] grew up in Prague and lived there till 1967, when I moved to Norway and later to the United States, where I met Sara in cold, snowy upstate New York.

We visited Prague dozens of times after the 1989 Velvet Revolution as we built and ran our business, the International Leadership Institute. We fulfilled Sara's long-held dream when we lived full-time in Vinohrady from 2010-2013.

So many relatives, friends, business owners, co-workers, and students from Prague have been part of our lives over the decades. Prague and its people have given us so much that we can only say, "Thank you, Prague!"

TABLE OF CONTENTS

INTRODUCTION: WHO WE ARE AND WHAT WE LOVE ABOUT PRAGUE

There are many "returning to Prague" stories of one kind or another about those visitors who are making another nostalgic trip to the city. They all have one distinct thing in common: sooner or later, it dawns on them that the Prague they see on their return trip is more alluring, more enchanting, and more fascinating than Prague from their previous experience.

We [Prague-born Jarda and his wife, American-born, Sara] have been returning to Prague now for thirty-five years, and our story is not an exception in this regard.

Our returns started in the Spring of 1990, shortly after the collapse of totalitarian communism in East and Central Europe, when I [Jarda] returned to Prague to visit my parents who had lived their whole lives there. It was my first trip to my native city since 1967, when I left Prague for Oslo, Norway.

That year, 1967, had been the beginning of the process of liberalization of the communist regime and a precursor of Alexander Dubček's "socialism with human face" and the Prague Spring of 1968. As a student of law at Charles University of Prague, I was granted permission to leave for a year to study the institution of the Ombudsman (citizen's defender) at the University of Oslo in Norway. I was interested in finding a solution to the problems of bureaucracy in the democratic society that I, along with others who were seeking a more open political landscape, envisioned in the future of Czechoslovakia.

So it was that just a year before the Soviet-led invasion of Czechoslovakia in August 1968, I went to Norway and began the process of learning the language, studying at the university, and supporting myself financially. I intended to return to Charles University and get my law degree, but after the Soviet invasion of my country, I decided to emigrate to the U.S.A. This was a long-held dream—to live in the country that had rescued Europe in WWII. I found a way, with the help of many kind people and supportive institutions, to become established in the United States.

A few years later, I became a naturalized U.S. citizen, which meant I could not go back to Czechoslovakia, as I would be branded as a traitor and most likely imprisoned. What started as a year away from my family and friends in Prague became two decades of "exile." It was not until the total collapse of the communist system there in 1989 that I returned to Prague.

In April 1990, when I finally arrived again in Prague, I was very glad to see my parents in their home. But I was very sad to see Domažlická Street in Žižkov, where I grew up. I could hardly believe my eyes at how much the street had deteriorated since 1967. It was beyond recognition and reminded me of the infamous Warsaw Pact era's "tankodroms"—tank training areas in the mud fields. There were no trees, and it was very challenging to cross the street without falling into a deep, muddy pit which became for me the symbol of the communist era.

It took my father's initiative to escort my mother and me on a tour of historic Prague, about which he was an expert. Only there, I started to see Prague in alluring, enchanting, and fascinating terms. Much of historical Prague was still well preserved, restored, or renovated, as the communist government needed showpieces to boost its image. An additional bonus was that there were almost no cars, as the average person couldn't afford one.

During those early days after the Velvet Revolution, as President Václav Havel was being installed in Hradčany Castle of Prague, Prague was just awakening from a forty-year slumber. Crumbling buildings sat next to well-preserved landmarks; the communist leaders were proud of Prague's past glory but had little desire to give everyday citizens a life that rose above grime, air pollution, and limited opportunity to travel or enlarge their vision of the world.

Prague is, of course, far more than the sum of its various physical parts, or its history, or its unique topography of palaces, churches, synagogues, architectural treasures, parks, squares, and streets. Each of our returns [Sara and me] between 1990 - 2025 has been memorable in new and unexpected ways. Yet some aspects of Prague's more-than-a-millennium-long history were present during each of our visits, and therefore we cover in this publication "Historical Prague" not as a separate chapter but in the districts we describe.

Sara and I are focusing on several aspects of Prague with which we are most familiar. They include historical Prague, architectural Prague, Prague of green spaces, residential Prague, and contemplative places in Prague. Historical Prague is covered mostly in chapters three, four, five, and six. Architectural Prague comes up in chapters one through six, and Prague of green spaces is the subject of chapters one, two, and seven. Quiet sanctuaries in the big city are described in chapter eight.

Clearly, it is Prague's more-than-a-millennium-long history, including the city's many upheavals and regime changes, which has made Prague a unique city of historical stability in the midst of turmoil.

In this book we hope to provide some relevant context for the millions of tourists that flock to the city each year, and entice you, the reader, to explore at least some of those inspiring places we are mentioning in this brief guide. We also hope to convey the excitement and anticipation we feel every time we visit Prague.

From Libuše's prophesy of "I see a great city whose glory will reach to the stars," immortalized in Bedřich Smetana's opera, "Libuše" (which is based on a legend of the eighth century A.D.), to the twenty-first century marked by a new, post-communist bustling city, Prague has drawn people from all over the world to experience something of the magnetism that continues to attract visitors.

May we invite you to join us and wander with us on a personal odyssey that will enable you to experience something of the city's stormy past and its dynamic present, as well as its unique essence?

Jaroslav and Sara Tusek
Winter Springs, Florida
May 2026

PS: if you want to discover more about Prague, you can find Sara's novel, *Prague for Beginners*, on Amazon. For a glimpse of our work in the

International Leadership Institute with business and government leaders in Central and Eastern Europe, you can also find on Amazon our experiences in leadership development in our book, *Leaders to Follow*.

CHAPTER ONE: THE FOUR GEMS OF VINOHRADY

Living in Prague from the 1940s through 1960s, it became clear to me [Jarda] that Prague is a living museum that documents the history of Central Europe from the eighth century to our times.

The story of Vinohrady details how the small, historical villages on the outskirts of Prague were gradually transformed into integral districts of the city. Vinohrady is a prime example of the rapid development of the city of Prague during the last two centuries.

Sara and I lived in Vinohrady from 2010-2013 and fell in love with its tree-lined streets and parks. It was a neighborhood I [Jarda] was familiar with since my youth because my aunt and uncle lived on quiet Dykova Street, known best for its cherry orchard. I often visited their residence, especially between 1945-1957.

Vinohrady has a convenient location, with good public transportation to the city center, which is only ten minutes away. Most recently, what we found very helpful in Vinohrady was the proximity of some of Prague's best and most reliable real estate firms. During 2025-2026, we especially benefited from the competent services provided to us through Mr. Adam Průša of HVB Real Estate, who helped us accomplish our real estate goals while satisfying the needs of all parties involved in complicated international real estate transactions.

Through our business, the International Leadership Institute, we've been leading tours of Prague for Americans and visitors from all over the world from 1990 through 2013, and we've found that Vinohrady is as good a district as any for starting an insightful tour of our favorite places in Prague. Let's get going!

The Four Gems of Vinohrady

From the tenth to fourteenth centuries, the Czech Kingdom developed into a prosperous electorate in the Holy Roman Empire, and Prague became a major trading and ecclesiastical center with significant German, Polish, and Jewish communities.

Vinohrady, one of the great treasures of the city, was established in those times as a village on the outskirts of Prague. Initially, a royal vineyard was established there in the fourteenth century by King of Bohemia and Holy Roman Emperor Charles IV, who required vineyards within a certain radius of Prague Castle (Vinohrady means "vineyards of the castle").

In the nineteenth century, Vinohrady evolved from agricultural land marked by vineyards and orchards. The village began to undergo rapid development in the nineteenth century, spurred by the construction of railways and the dismantling of Prague's city walls. It became a popular area for the wealthy to live and a center for intellectuals and artists.

New streets, squares, schools, theaters, businesses, churches, and spacious parks were established, and Vinohrady quickly gained a reputation for its elegant atmosphere, diverse architectural styles, and beautiful spacious parks like Riegrovy sady or Grébovka. Vinohrady became a popular residential area with its beauty and proximity to the city center.

Now, it is best known for its spectacular design and vibrant cultural scene. The district's residential area is favored by Americans and expats from the EU countries. It boasts a great mix of architectural styles including Neo-Renaissance, Art Nouveau, and neo-Gothic, especially from the late nineteenth and early twentieth centuries. Cafes, restaurants, art galleries, entertainment venues, and the ornate Vinohrady Theatre all are on offer in Vinohrady,

The district has two main squares: Náměstí Míru, centered on the neo-Gothic Church of St. Ludmila, and Náměstí Jiřího z Poděbrad Square (JZP), based around the Church of Most Sacred Heart of Our Lord, which was built in 1932 by architect Jože Plečnik from Ljubljana, Slovenia. This church is a mixture of architectural styles with contemporary, classical, and Gothic elements.

Although both Sara and I have lived in quite a few cities, rural areas, and small towns in Europe and the U.S, we loved our years on Lužická street in Vinohrady in a special way. The quiet of the tree-canopied street made it truly a hidden gem. We were close to a busy shopping street and minutes from Václavské náměstí (Wenceslas Square), but we felt like we were nestled in a secluded village. Near us were parks, churches, and schools, giving us plenty of choices for walking our miniature Dachshund, Klaus!

With its excellent transportation links and closeness to Prague's center, Vinohrady is an ideal place from which to begin your explorations of Prague. We will focus on four unique places that we call the “gems” of Vinohrady.

The First Gem of Vinohrady: Grébovka Park (Havlíčkovy sady)

It took less than a century for Vinohrady to gain its reputation as one of the most desirable residential districts in Prague. One fashionable neighborhood near Havlíčkovy sady has contributed greatly to the overall fame of the Vinohrady district. Locals often call Havlíčkovy sady “Grébovka,” after the grand Villa Grobe that stands overlooking Prague's first castle area, Vyšehrad, which was constructed in the tenth century.

Villa Grobe is a solid example of Neo-Renaissance architecture. Built as a luxury summer residence for industrialist Moritz Grobe in the late nineteenth century, the building stands in a gracefully landscaped, terraced garden at the head of a long slope. The slope is covered by a well-maintained vineyard with a gazebo at the top where you can sit and enjoy a glass of wine, or you can have coffee and snacks at a café near the villa. You can also have a decent meal at the adjoining Pavilion Grébovka Restaurant.

The large park, Havlíčkovy sady, features an artistic grotto, a waterfall with a pond, and an impressive variety of old trees. All year round, locals spend time there hiking its many paths, dog walking, picnicking, or just relaxing on one of the park's benches. Numerous public events such as the annual Wine Festival or Family Day take place in the park throughout the year.

Havlíčkovy sady and Grébovka are located about seven blocks from náměstí Míru, and it takes about ten minutes to walk from náměstí Míru to the park.

The Second Gem of Vinohrady: Hotel Orion

Only about three blocks from Havlíčkovy sady, on Americká Street, is the second Vinohrady gem, the charming, small family-run Hotel Orion. It's a pleasant, friendly, convenient, and reasonably-priced hotel of the O.K. group of hotels.

Hotel Orion is situated near náměstí Míru and is only a short tram ride from the city center. The founder of post-WWI Czechoslovakia, T.G. Masaryk, lived in a nearby villa, giving the area an extra historical significance.

Sara and I enjoy staying in this family-run hotel during our yearly visits to Prague. Hotel Orion provides a home-like atmosphere in apartments, from studios to family two-bedroom apartments and a roof-top luxury apartment with spectacular views of Prague Castle. The hotel has access to internet, cable TV, and daily maid service, as well as a quiet private courtyard where you can eat breakfast or enjoy the evening calm.

The hotel concierge service is available round the clock, providing assistance with travel arrangements, restaurant recommendations, discount coupons for local restaurants, laundry services, and directions for parking. It is an ideal base for exploring the district of Vinohrady without tourist crowds. Sara and I especially love the nearby cafes and restaurants which offer Vietnamese, vegan, Italian, Mexican, and Ukrainian food at prices much more affordable than in the center of Prague.

Hotel Orion has a fascinating history, dating back to the challenging times of the 1920s. The original owners built the house for their living quarters and for renting out apartments. They ran a small printing house on the ground floor and became successful entrepreneurs during the time of Vinohrady's growing popularity and reputation as a desirable residential area. The story of Hotel Orion reminds me [Jarda] of my grandparents' apartment house in Žižkov, which combined their small, handcrafted shoe factory with living accommodations.

The secret of Hotel Orion is its people. The friendly and hardworking multi-national, English-speaking staff are able and willing to help whenever you need something. The hands-on management team makes each guest feel special and is eager to help make your stay enjoyable and memorable.

Hotel Orion offers a range of convenient facilities to ensure a comfortable and hassle-free stay for its guests and provides an affordable alternative to staying in an expensive luxury hotel in the city center.

Address: Americká 9, Vinohrady

The Third Gem of Vinohrady: Vinohradská tržnice/ Pavilion (Vinohrady Market Hall)

Although the most well-known building on Vinohrady Street may be the Český rozhlas building (Czech Radio), the Vinohradská tržnice building comes as a close second. One of the three most venerated historic market halls in Prague, Vinohradská Tržnice is located just a few blocks down Vinohrady Street from Náměstí Jiřího z Poděbrad. It was built in 1902 by a leading Vinohrady architect of the time, Antonín Turek. The building was declared a cultural monument and thus spared demolition during the communist totalitarian era.

Vinohradská tržnice was completely reconstructed in 1995 in the hopes of creating a popular and convenient shopping center. However, the market hall did not draw in enough customers and needed to be repurposed for the twenty-first century.

Fortunately for the building, in 2012 Martin Leithgeber came up with an idea to reconstruct it again into an exhibition and market hall for modern furniture and arts. This has significantly increased the importance and popularity of the building and stopped its gradual deterioration.

This imaginative transformation earns the building's significance as the third of our four jewels of Vinohrady. The last (but not least of the four jewels) is Riegrovy sady, which we will describe briefly next.

The Fourth Gem of Vinohrady: Riegrovy sady (Rieger's Orchards)

When I [Jarda] was growing up in Prague, 1941-1967, this park was my favorite place for sports, recreation, relaxation, and enjoying inspiring and memorable views of Petřín Hill and Hradčany Castle on the other side of the Vltava River.

Riegrovy sady is a park which is relatively hidden from tourist crowds in spite of its closeness to nearby Wenceslas Square. As with so many parks, buildings, churches, and monuments in Prague, Riegrovy sady's character has changed over the centuries.

The park was built in the twentieth century on the site of former vineyards established during the Holy Roman Emperor Charles IV's reign. The vineyards had been destroyed during the Thirty Years' War in the seventeenth century.

The park, built on a hillside, boasts fairy-tale, classic views of Prague's Hradčany castle, Malá Strana (The Lesser Town), and Staré Město (the Old Town).

In Riegrovy sady, there is a late Classicist building which now houses a café and an observation tower called Mlékárna (The Milk House). The park is also known for the well-established sporting grounds of Vinohrady Sokol (with a track and field stadium and a swimming pool), a restaurant which offers international cuisine, and a large, popular beer garden. Locals and tourists alike enjoy the park's classic English garden design setting, which is ideal for picnics, relaxation, sports, and recreational activities as well as walks and runs.

This park extends all the way to charming Rajská zahrada (The Paradise Garden) in Žižkov, known for its beautiful waterfall and a pond full of wildlife, including turtles. This garden is covered in the next chapter.

Riegrovy sady offers numerous benches to take a break from your adventures in Prague. Flower beds, trees, and woody plants abound in the park. It is a superb alternative to a day of hectic sightseeing because of its relaxing and refreshing atmosphere.

CHAPTER TWO: FUN TIMES IN ŽIŽKOV

Good morning, lucky visitor to Žižkov. I [Jarda] am one of Žižkov's native sons. A bit more earthy than Vinohrady, and with a working-class background, Žižkov has been a stronghold of the Hussite heritage of Bohemian and Czech history.

As I write this brief chapter on the quirky places to see in Žižkov, I can't help thinking of all those great Czech writers and poets who've made Prague famous. I am talking about writers like František Palacký and his *History of the Czech Nation*; Jan Neruda with his *Stories of Malá Strana* and his famous "fejetony" (short, witty commentary); Franz Kafka's *Josef K.*; Jaroslav Seifert's *Mozart in Prague* and his poems about Prague; and Karel

Čapek with his battle cry in defense of freedom, *Matka*.

These literary greats preferred to see in Prague only its golden attributes and wrote about the city as Matka (Mother) Praha. They rarely seem to have discovered anything sinister or imagined dark secrets in their insights into Prague; they have mostly avoided tragic subjects. But writer Jaroslav Hašek saw the "claws" in the city. His comic novel *The Good Soldier Schweik (Švejk* in Czech) and many of his great short stories take place in Žižkov's pubs, squares, and streets, as well as in the jails where Josef Švejk and his companions met.

Growing up in Žižkov, I discovered Žižkov's claws in the schools I attended, in the sport grounds, in Žižkov's town hall, and in other public offices during the communist totalitarian era. These claws were sharp; they would quickly punish anyone who stepped out of line.

Since that time, however, Žižkov has been gradually transformed into a more relaxed neighborhood which is growing increasingly popular for students and young people from the EU countries, the U.K, the U.S, and Canada. Žižkov is being gentrified at a fast pace as it benefits from its three spacious green parks: Vítkov Hill, Parukářka sady, and Rajská zahrada (Paradise Garden). Another large green space in Žižkov is provided by Olšanské hřbitovy (the Olšany cemeteries).

Žižkov should be on your list if you want to get at least a little bit familiar with the more eclectic, vibrant, honest, and authentic face of Prague. There are many independent shops, quirky cafés, restaurants, and bars with vibrant nightlife. You can come to Žižkov for fun and to escape the tourist crowds in the city's center.

Žižkov's TV Tower is visible from pretty much everywhere in Prague, standing tall among the hills to the east of the Old Town. This quarter also has some surprisingly old historical sites like the Starý židovský hřbitov (Old Jewish Cemetery) founded in 1680.

Following are several places I can highly recommend for an enjoyable visit to this unique Prague district. Let us start with the TV Tower and then proceed to Parukářka sady on the Holy Cross Hill, the National Monument on Vítkov Hill, Škroupovo náměstí, the Paradise Garden, and the Old Jewish Cemetery.

Fun Times in Žižkov: TV Tower

The "towering" tower is not just the tallest building in Prague. It's also the highest observation point in the Czech Republic, climbing to 216 meters, or 683 feet tall, in Mahlerovy sady, the green space surrounding it.

The tower was not naïvely conceived by "an innocent and peaceful" communist regime. On the pretext of significantly improving television reception, the TV tower was actually designed to throw a giant blanket of reception obstruction over the whole region, jamming Western European airwave transmissions, specifically Austrian and West German television signals.

Now it serves as an observation tower; the viewing areas on all sides offer magnificent views of Prague, and on a clear day with good visibility, even the Giant Mountains in the northern part of Czech Republic can be seen. The tower has two high-speed elevators, a restaurant, and a snack bar open for late breakfast.

After viewing Parukářka sady from the top of the tower, it's a good time to visit Holy Cross Hill, which is located about twenty minutes' walk from the tower.

Fun Times in Žižkov: Holy Cross Hill and Parukářka sady

The whole of Holy Cross Hill was originally covered with vineyards founded by Emperor Charles IV of the Holy Roman Empire in the fourteenth century. The park is called "Parukářka" (the Wig), most likely because one of the prominent houses located there belonged to Jan Hrabal, a well-known Prague wigmaker.

During my childhood [Jarda], Holy Cross Hill was my favorite playground, close to our home on Domažlická street. I also spent many hours there in the early 1950s as a volunteer participant in cleaning up the park to repair the damage done during the May 1945 Prague Uprising against the Nazi occupiers in WWII.

Holy Cross Hill offers memorable views of Prague, and the park offers refreshment stalls, a pub, and a large children's playground. From the park, it's about twenty minutes' walk to The National Memorial Building on Vítkov Hill.

Fun Times in Žižkov: Vítkov Hill and the National Memorial Building

The National Memorial Building was constructed during the First Republic (1918-1938) in honor of the Czech legionnaires of WWI. Vítkov Hill is, at about 330 meters high, one of the highest points in the city. From the building at the crest of the hill, you will see great views of most of Prague.

In front of the National Memorial Building is a twenty-two-meter (approximately seventy-two feet) tall statue of Hussite military leader Jan Žižka of Trocnov on horseback. One of the most important battles of the Hussite wars took place on Vítkov Hill in 1420, fought between the Hussite defenders and the crusader Catholic forces assembled from all over Europe by King Sigismund of Hungary. Žižka and his Hussite warriors soundly defeated King Sigismund's crusade.

The equestrian statue of Žižka commemorates the Hussites' victory, which resulted in their playing a significant role in the history of Protestantism in Europe. More than one hundred years before Martin Luther's activities, Bohemian theologian and philosopher Jan Hus attempted to reform the Roman Catholic church of the fourteenth century in Prague, which led to the Hussite Revolution and wars in the fifteenth century.

Fun Times in Žižkov: Škroupovo náměstí

This is a round-shaped “square” with a little park, named after the composer František Škroup. The square earned its reputation by being the site of the first officially permitted demonstration by opposition groups during the period of so-called "normalization" after the August 1968 Soviet-led invasion of Czechoslovakia.

Prague 3 (Žižkov) Mayor Jiří Ptáček recalled the event. “Basically, the only anti-regime demonstration allowed during the communist era in our country was in Škroupovo náměstí on Saturday, Dec. 10, 1988. The original plan to obtain a permit for Václavák (Václavské náměstí/Wenceslas Square) did not work out. It was banned under the pretext of protecting monuments. The organizers tried Prague 3 and obtained permission from the local ONV,” Ptáček said.

This peaceful demonstration took place on the anniversary of the adoption of the Universal Declaration of Human Rights. Future president of Czechoslovakia Václav Havel spoke at the event. Historian Petr Blažek says Havel's speech was characteristic of the entire demonstration: "He came across as quite shy, and it wasn't that convincing. But on the other hand, the very fact he could speak in Prague at a public meeting for the first time in twenty years or so was, of course, a major change."

An estimated crowd of two to three thousand people turned up for the gathering. Some regime opponents had stayed away out of fear of the usual riot police violence. Others only heard about the hastily-agreed event when it was over. The repercussions of the protest would become part of the November 1989 Velvet Revolution that overthrew the communist government.

Now the square provides a relaxing and pleasant place to sit and watch the world go by. It's close to Žižkov's TV Tower, and it's a short walk to our next recommended destination, Rajská zahrada (The Paradise Garden).

Fun Times in Žižkov: Rajská zahrada (Paradise Garden)

This park is one of Žižkov's newest green spaces, in the middle of the district. Paradise Garden is a charming and well-hidden park located near Riegrovy sady, offering a peaceful escape from Žižkov's bustle.

We recommend this place because of its tranquil atmosphere, with a beautiful, long man-made waterfall, a pond with fish and turtles, and children's playgrounds, making it great for families. There is also a pleasant cafe with classic views of Prague's Hradčany Castle.

The park hosts various events, including concerts, exhibitions, festivals, and outdoor movie screenings during summer months. It also offers wonderful scenic vistas from its elevated position in the center of Žižkov amidst flower gardens and nature. It's a perfect spot for a leisurely walk, to relax with children, to enjoy a quiet moment, or to take a few memorable pictures,

Fun Times in Žižkov: Starý židovský hřbitov na Žižkově (Old Jewish Cemetery)

One warm evening, I [Sara] took a stroll after eating in one of our favorite Greek restaurants. I had no destination and allowed myself to get pleasantly lost on the back streets of Žižkov.

As I turned a corner, I saw a dark, mysterious lane that ended in a thick stucco wall. Intrigued, I walked down and found tall, wrought-iron gates securely locked. I looked in and could only make out, very dimly, white shapes in the shadows.

Then I saw a sign on the wall: "Starý židovský hřbitov." These were three Czech words I knew: Old Jewish Cemetery. The atmosphere of the cemetery, an enigmatic blend of secrets and peace, is something I have never forgotten.

When I got back home, I did some research and found that this cemetery was established in 1680 as a burial place for plague victims from the Prague Jewish community. The Old Jewish Cemetery in Josefov had become too crowded. The Jewish community bought this plot of land in Žižkov to bury those who had died of the plague

From 1787 to 1890, the Žižkov cemetery was the most important Jewish burial place in Prague. Forty thousand people were buried here — rabbis, scholars, leading Prague industrialists, bankers, and other famous (and less famous) people of the Jewish community.

When in 1890, the Žižkov Jewish cemetery was full, the New Jewish Cemetery in Vinohrady took over its function.

In the 1980s, the Žižkov town council decided to convert about three-fourths of the cemetery into a public park, Mahlerovy sady. Another part of the cemetery was badly devastated between 1985 and 1986 during the excavation of the foundations for the communist-era construction of the Žižkov TV

Tower. Now only the oldest part with the most valuable tombstones survives.

One fascinating recent addition to this cemetery is the Return of the Stones (Návrat kamenů). This is a memorial made of some six thousand broken headstones of Jewish graves. These headstones had been used in 1987 (after the destruction of most of the cemetery) as cobblestones to pave Wenceslas Square.

When the square was renovated in 2020, the cobblestones were handed over to the Jewish community, which commissioned the artists Jaroslav and Lucie Rona to create a memorial. They built a mound surrounded by nine blocks made up of the cobblestones. Hebrew and Roman alphabets can be seen on some of the stones.

In so many ways, the Starý židovský hřbitov na Žižkově still provides an important witness of the key role of Prague's Jewish community in the history of Prague.

The first two-and-a-half decades of my life [Jarda] were spent in Žižkov. Its unique flavor of sharp contrasts and colorful characters has enfolded me into its story as it has evolved from a place of fields and pastures in the nineteenth century to its modern status as an earthy and somewhat gritty Prague neighborhood.

If you want to see an authentic Žižkov pub, where the regulars all know each other's stories and may have a singalong if the spirit moves them, or if you want to hike up Vítkov Hill among the trees, or if you simply want to get a glimpse of life in a place that's slowly changing while retaining its unique appeal, then Žižkov is the place for you.

As you've walked the streets and parks of Žižkov, you've undoubtedly noticed the castle in the distance. Now is a good time to jump on a tram and travel across the Vltava River to Hradčany, the castle complex at the beating heart of the Bohemian kingdom.

You'll need your walking shoes, because the complex with its surrounding gardens, villas, museums, palaces, and squares spreads across hilly land, and the cobblestoned lanes can be a footwear challenge.

CHAPTER THREE: GOING TO THE CASTLE—HRADČANY

My first visit to Prague, in 1990, [Sara] was full of amazing and fascinating sights. But the one place that made my jaw drop open was Hradčany.

For me as an American, castles are monuments to ambition and power, usually built on solitary hilltops to proclaim their dominance over the surrounding countryside and rivers. Castles defend, protect, and honor the royalty who live within.

In this regard, Prague Castle (Hradčany) exemplifies all a castle can be and then some, with many added features that have accumulated over eleven centuries. Built on a hilltop overlooking the Vltava River, with palaces, civic buildings, residences, churches, salons, gardens, lanes, and towers enclosed in sturdy walls, Hradčany is both impressive and educational.

You won't see all of Hradčany in a day, so get a map and choose highlights that appeal to you. I lived in Prague for three years but never saw every nook and cranny of Prague Castle. It's so easy to get caught up in the splendor and majesty of the architecture and gardens that you lose track of time and later realize how much more there is to see.

In our two previous books on Prague (*Prague For Beginners* and *Three Things You Can't do in Prague*), we wrote about various aspects of "going to the castle" in more detail. Here, we are giving a quick overview.

I [Jarda] have been going to the castle for decades, ever since my childhood in Prague. My introduction to the castle began with my grandmother, who took me there regularly. She showed me the historical sites and stirred my interest in the long, evolving story of Hradčany. Every visit included the fifteenth-century Golden Lane, which is highlighted later in this chapter.

We always find a visit to Hradčany Castle to be refreshing, inspiring, and a new learning experience. We recognize the central and crucial role that the castle has played throughout the nation's and the city's history. As the complex includes government buildings and offices in daily use, struggles for civil rights and political power are still taking place at Prague castle.

Note: Just to make things a bit more confusing, the neighborhood around the Hradčany complex is also called Hradčany. If you ask to be taken to Hradčany, you may get a question: which one?

Going to the Castle—Hradčany: The Castle Complex

Hradčany is not a castle as you may think of castles: one monumental building standing alone, a romantic sentinel on the crest of a rocky hill.

Instead, it's a high-walled complex enclosing courtyards, passageways, dozens of buildings and gardens, lanes, towers, and stairways that have been added during more than a millennium of the history of the Czech state.

Approaching the castle is a bit of an adventure. First-time visitors to Hradčany may not be sure exactly where to enter the complex. Here, a map will help—free maps are readily available in hotels and tourist offices.

The main entry to the castle complex is on Hradčanské náměstí (Hradčany Square), with its imposing border of grand houses and palaces built by Bohemian nobles wishing to be close to the castle.

The sculpture-laden gateway, flanked by two light-blue uniformed Castle Guards standing in their striped sentry boxes, leads you into a large, paved courtyard surrounded by thick walls and anonymous-looking buildings. Your castle map can help you identify the buildings while giving you a bit of their history.

There are a few other ways into the complex: climb up a steep flight of steps (the Castle Stairs) from the Malostranská station metro stop or take Tram 22 to the stop called Pražský hrad, then walk across a short pedestrian bridge.

Going to the Castle—Hradčany: St. Vitus Cathedral

To explore Hradčany castle in all its glory would take several visits, but the most famous buildings are in or close to the courtyard that holds St. Vitus Cathedral (Katedrála svatého Víta, Václava a Vojtěcha).

The dominant building in the castle complex, the Gothic cathedral sitting in unquestionable majesty in the middle of a huge stone courtyard, is St. Vitus Cathedral. The building has changed significantly in the millennium since it was founded, and its importance (spiritual, historical, and civic) has grown with the changes. Czech kings and queens took part of coronation services on this site, and patron saints, sovereigns, noblemen, and archbishops are interred in the underground crypt.

Around the year 925, Prince Wenceslas (Václav) built the first church on this site, a Romanesque rotunda. In 1344, Holy Roman Emperor and King of Bohemia Charles IV, as part of his grand project of modernizing and expanding the area we know as Prague, began the construction of a Gothic cathedral on the site.

As with such projects all over Europe, work on the building was slow and was often paused for many years as wars, changing architectural styles, and economic and political disruptions had their effect. The church was finally completed and consecrated in 1929, as the new country of Czechoslovakia was celebrating its freedom and prosperity after its creation at the end of WWI.

Today you can tour the cathedral and see its splendors: the silver tomb of Jan Nepomuk with an army of angels supporting a canopy, the coronation chamber with the crown jewels, Wenceslas Chapel with wall paintings depicting the saint's life, and tall stained-glass windows designed by Art Nouveau painter and decorative artist Alfons Mucha.

The cathedral is still a functioning house of worship, so be aware that there may be services under way. You can visit the website of St. Vitus Cathedral (Katedrála svatého Víta, Václava a Vojtěcha) to gain information about the eventful history of the cathedral and its current activities and events. Special times are set aside for visitors.

About two million visitors come to see the cathedral's remarkable interior each year. The vastness and richness of decoration and furnishings that meet your eyes in the cathedral may dazzle you, and the impressive history of the cathedral's service to the people of Prague may help you better understand the age and high culture of Prague.

Going to the Castle—Hradčany: a walk around the complex

As you cross the vast courtyard in which St. Vitus Cathedral takes pride of place, you see ahead of you St. George's Basilica, my favorite part of the castle complex [Sara].

St. George's Basilica (Bazilika sv. Jiří) is the oldest surviving church building within the castle complex; it was founded by Vratislaus I of Bohemia in 920. Its low, simple, rosy-orange Romanesque exterior is a complete contrast to the Gothic heights of St. Vitus Cathedral. The plain interior, with no carved pews or ornate statues, has stone walls, a modest altar, and faded frescoes that take me back to another millennium. With St. George's Convent next door, built in 973, the spiritual beginnings of Prague are evident.

Golden Lane

If you walk through the castle complex past St. Vitus Cathedral and St. George's Basilica, you find yourself on a narrow, cobbled street. Down a bit on the left is Golden Lane, a picturesque collection of miniature, colorful houses built one against the next. Home to workers in the castle, especially marksmen and goldsmiths, this fifteenth-century lane later became a haven for artists and writers. Franz Kafka lived at No 22 for a while. It is now a bookshop and contains a tiny Kafka museum.

Going to the Castle—Hradčany: The Royal Town of Hradčany

The entire castle complex is popularly known as Hradčany; this is also the name of the town that began to grow in the fourteenth century outside the castle walls.

Castles need a community to support their needs for construction, maintenance, defense, transportation, and keeping the peace. The inhabitants need food and clothing, household furnishings, and the latest fashions. It's logical, then, that a village of workers will spring to life around the castle.

In its earliest form, Hradčany was the smallest of the Prague towns. King of Bohemia and Holy Roman Emperor Charles IV later enlarged the town walls. Hradčany is still a small neighborhood with notable squares such as Loreto (Loretánské náměstí), the home of the Baroque Church of the

Nativity and a pilgrimage site connected to the Virgin Mary.

Nový Svět

Take a stroll across Hradčany Square and follow the little streets to a lovely corner and street known as Nový Svět (New World). First occupied around 1320, this area was made up of dwellings for people who worked for the Royal Court but were not considered important enough to live closer to the castle.

Three fires and frequent changes in the population of Nový Svět meant that its reputation rose and fell with the years. Now it's a quiet, hidden place to hear bird song across a walled garden and imagine you are in a village far from the city.

Going to the Castle—Hradčany: Strahov Monastery (Strahovský klášter)

Founded in 1140, the monastery complex is situated on the Hradčany heights overlooking the Vltava River. Strahov offers a collection of buildings in a range of ages, purposes, and architectural styles as well as outstanding views of the city of Prague.

There are two churches in the monastery walls: one, dedicated to St. Roch, was donated by Emperor Rudolf II in 1603 in gratitude for being spared from the plague. Since the twentieth century, it has served as an exhibition hall. The second is the impressive Basilica of the Assumption of the Virgin Mary, remodeled in Baroque style in the eighteenth century.

Not to be missed are the Strahov Library with medieval manuscripts, maps, and globes; the Baroque Theological Hall; the Classical Philosophy Hall (decorated with frescoes); and the Strahov

Gallery with its collections of Gothic paintings, Rudolfian art, and Baroque and Rococo paintings.

A decent restaurant with outdoor seating and the venerable Strahov brewery, making St. Norbert beer since the thirteenth century, offer food and drink for the weary.

On a warm afternoon, you can sit outside and see, spread at your feet, an orchard and a park (complete with lanovka, the funicular railway up and down) tumbling down toward the Vltava River. Lifting your eyes, you have a spectacular view of Charles Bridge, the Old Town Square, and the hills surrounding Prague.

Strahov is always bustling, but it also offers quiet corners for imagining yourself living there nine centuries ago. The mixture of religious tradition with closeness to the Hradčany castle insures that Strahov remains an important part of the town of Hradčany.

CHAPTER FOUR: MALÁ STRANA (LESSER TOWN)

If I [Sara] had to choose my favorite part of Prague, it would be Malá Strana.

I love its lively energy and mingled eras of architecture: tiny, everyday shops and cafes in medieval buildings; aristocratic gardens; monumental churches; tram tracks embedded in cobble-stoned squares; the fun tunnel where Tram 22 passes within inches of the walls of Saint Thomas Church (Kostel svatého Tomáše); and the ever-changing views of Hradčany and its hillside royal gardens as you turn a corner.

The first time I crossed Charles Bridge into Malá Strana from the Old Town, I was puzzled by the crush of archways, buildings, and towers that marked this entrance. In contrast to the solitary Gothic tower at the Old Town entrance of the bridge, the Malá Strana end of the bridge is a hodgepodge of architectural styles of different heights and purposes.

This entrance is a good metaphor for all of Malá Strana, a district with a complicated history and a variety of people living at close quarters. Above all, the hilly terrain and highly-sought-after small, flat area on the bank of the Vltava River have shaped the function and growth of this unique part of Prague.

Winding, cobbled alleyways; hidden stone stairs from one level to the next; private walled gardens; bustling narrow streets full of shoppers and sidewalk cafes; and easy access to Hradčany make Malá Strana as charming a place as you can imagine.

As over the centuries, the Hradčany castle complex was constantly being expanded, rebuilt, and modernized, the people whose labor and imagination were crucial to the process lived nearby, surrounding the castle complex. On narrow, crooked streets and stone-laid squares, the activities of tradespeople from Germany, Italy, and the surrounding Bohemian countryside created the diverse district known as the Malá Strana—the "Lesser Town."

As Malá Strana grew, it attracted wealthy nobles and merchants as well as artisans. Many of the aristocrats built elaborate homes in the shadow of Hradčany, getting reflected glory from the hilltop castle. Their palaces and gardens are still there, many of them open to the public.

In this chapter are a few of our most-loved places in Malá Strana. By no means do we cover all the historical sites, but instead we focus on showing you both the lavish and the human, daily sides of this fascinating part of Prague.

Malá Strana: Neruda Street (Nerudova ulice)

On my first visit to Prague in 1990, no sooner had Jarda and I [Sara] walked across Charles Bridge and under the stone archway into Malá Strana than he whisked me past shops and through Malostranské náměstí, a big, anonymous-looking square, into Nerudova Street.

I looked up at the steep climb to the top of the narrow street and wondered what awaited us there. By this time, though, I had learned that Jarda had his own way of doing things, so I trusted him that whatever he showed me would be worth the effort.

We quickly trekked uphill past wooden doors every few feet. They all looked the same to me: badly in need of a coat of paint and completely unreadable. Was it a shop? A restaurant? Someone's apartment or miniscule house? The doors had no numbers or markings on them.

Then I noticed the old, scarred wooden signs that hung above some doors. One sign had three carved violins; this was, I found out later, a famous restaurant where we often ate in later years.

We hustled past these intriguing signs and blank-faced doors to the top, where the street made a hairpin bend to the right. Still ascending, we followed a ramp that suddenly blossomed into a big open space, Hradčanské Square. And here it was: the castle.

In those days, there were no guards in pretty, light-blue uniforms, and the castle entrance was more intimidating than welcoming. We took a brisk walk through the complex and exited via the Old Castle Steps, back down to the metro station and Tram 22.

We visited Neruda Street many times after that, taking time to look at the signs such as "Two Suns" where Czech writer Jan Neruda had lived. I remember vividly stepping into a tiny hole-in-the-wall pub, no more than twelve feet wide, with a ceiling stained yellowish-brown by cigarettes, cigars, and pipes over the centuries.

This no-name pub had a few tables where about a dozen older men sat in comfortable silence, having a beer together as they had probably done for many years. I felt like we were walking into someone's chata (weekend cabin), as everyone else knew each other, and we were total strangers. We had a quick beer and left them to their memories.

Malá Strana: American Embassy and Petřín Hill

Tucked away on a side street, the American Embassy occupies the former Schoenborn Palace at Tržiště 365/15. Among the past owners of the palace were Cardinal Prince Dietrichstein; Count Rudolph Colloredo; Charles, Count of Hatzfeld; The Prince of Hatzfeld; and Count Schoenborn. Franz Kafka also lived in the palace briefly in 1917.

The building is noteworthy not for its interior, which is full of offices as you would expect, but because of its setting. Behind the palace stretches a terraced garden and orchard of seven acres which extends up a hillside topped by the Glorietta, from which the American flag flies.

This garden leads to Petřín Hill. We have written about Petřín Hill in the "Green Spaces" chapter, along with Vrtba Garden, which is behind the American Embassy.

Malá Strana: Maltese Square (Maltézské náměstí)

Maltese Square is the location of the Church of Our Lady beneath the Chain (Kostel Panny Marie pod řetězem), built by the Knights of Malta in the twelfth century. The church's name reflects the fact that the Knights used a chain to block boats on the nearby Vltava River to ensure they paid customs duties.

Malá Strana is not a large district. You can walk most of it in a morning or afternoon, stopping along the way for a quick lunch from the daily lunch menu (denní menu) in any traditional restaurant. These lunches cost around 150-300 CZK (approx. $7–$14 USD), often including soup. Common options include traditional Czech meat-based cuisine like goulash, schnitzel, or svíčková.

Leaving Malá Strana by crossing Charles Bridge leads you to the Old Town, which we cover in the next chapter.

CHAPTER FIVE: STARÉ MĚSTO (OLD TOWN)

Prague's historical centerpiece is Civitas Pragensis--The Old Town of Prague, or in Czech, "Staré Město." It is the key settlement in Czech history and has stayed remarkably unchanged since the Middle Ages. Not only has the Old Town been able to keep its individual character and charm, but its flexibility has allowed it to remain a living neighborhood rather than a tired museum.

When I [Sara] first visited Prague in 1990, I fell in love with the Old Town. Its winding, narrow, cobblestoned streets beckoned me. Within minutes of entering the Old Town, I was pleasantly lost and completely absorbed with the buildings illustrating a variety of architectural periods, and with the small cafés and shops hidden in recessed doorways.

The combination of tiny, private-seeming streets that suddenly open out into large squares and boulevards gives the Old Town a particularly unpredictable charm. Gustav Meyrink's novel *The Golem* captures this fairy-tale quality of the Old Town in a dreamlike story of ancient Jewish kabalistic myth. The mystical air of the Old Town, especially at night, draws you under its spell.

At the same time, though, any settlement this old has its dark moments in history. In 1621, after they had lost the Battle of White Mountain, twenty-seven leaders of the Bohemian Estates Uprising (a Protestant rebellion against Catholic Habsburg rule) were publicly executed by the Habsburg victors in the Old Town Square.

Twelve of their heads were put into iron baskets and attached by the executioner to Charles Bridge, where they hung until the invasion by the Saxon army took place in 1631, at the start of the Thirty Years' War.

Czech collective memory has never forgiven the victorious Habsburgs for this massacre of its nobility. When I [Jarda] played power volleyball in the Czech Republic during the 1960s, my team's rallying cry before a match was "Za Bílou horu!" This cry invoked the Battle of White Mountain as a source of strength and determination to win the match.

The Old Town hides its past among its lanes, old market squares, and alleyways. The best way to get to know it is to take a few hours, at least, to wander at a slow pace and absorb the atmosphere created by centuries of daily life.

Staré Město (Old Town): An open-air living museum

The Old Town can be seen as a "skanzen", an open-air living museum showcasing more than a millennium of continuous urban development from the ninth and tenth centuries: first as a busy marketplace at the crossroads of several European trade routes, then as a cultural, commercial, educational, and religious Central European center in medieval times, and today as a must-see for tourists and visitors from all over the world.

The architectural highlights of the Old Town include the historic Gothic, Baroque, and Renaissance buildings of Charles University of Prague, founded in 1348 by King of Bohemia and Holy Roman Emperor Charles IV; the former Jesuit college of Klementinum with its Astronomical Tower and Baroque Library; and the Rudolfinum, a Neo-Renaissance building completed in 1884 which is currently the home of the Czech Philharmonic Orchestra.

From the Rudolfinum you can see yet another perspective on the Hradčany complex, Petřín Hill, and Charles Bridge. The building is one of three major buildings on Jan Palach Square; the Faculty of Arts of Charles University, and the Academy of Arts, Architecture and Design are the other two.

Jan Palach Square was renamed after the 1989 Velvet Revolution to honor the student Jan Palach who immolated himself in January 1969 in protest against the 1968 Soviet invasion of Czechoslovakia.

From Jan Palach Square, it's a walk of just a few blocks to quiet Josefov, the traditional Jewish neighborhood off busy Pařížská Street. Once a walled ghetto, the only place where Jews could live in Prague, Josefov's history has had its ups and downs.

Staré Město (Old Town): Josefov

Jewish merchants settled in Prague beginning in the tenth century. In 1096, during the First Crusade, crusaders on the way to recapture the city of Jerusalem and the Holy Land from Muslim control entered Prague's Jewish quarter and murdered hundreds of Jews. Another attack on Jews in 1142 spurred the development of the walled ghetto, with doors locked at night. The ghetto both defended the Jewish settlers (who were forced to live there) and restricted their movements.

The Jewish community became prosperous towards the end of the 16th century when its mayor, Mordecai Maisel, became the Minister of Finance and a very wealthy man. His philanthropy helped develop the ghetto.

In 1850, the quarter was renamed Josefov (Joseph's City) after Josef II, Holy Roman Emperor who emancipated Jews with the Edict of Tolerance in

1782. Jews were allowed to settle outside the ghetto; mostly Orthodox and poor Jews continued living there.

Most of Josefov was demolished between 1893 and 1913 as part of an initiative to model the city of Prague to resemble the city of Paris. What was left were only six synagogues, the old cemetery, and the Old Jewish Town Hall.

We will talk more about the synagogues and cemetery in Chapter Eight, “Quiet Sanctuaries in the Big City.”

Staré Město (Old Town): Old Town Square (Staroměstské náměstí)

Every Prague tourist knows Old Town Square (Staroměstské náměstí), the "center of the center" of the Old Town. Famous landmarks there include the Astronomical Clock (Orloj) on City Hall, the two-towered Týn Cathedral (The Church of the Virgin Mary Before Týn/Týnský chrám), and the Art Nouveau sculpture of martyred Bohemian priest Jan Hus. At the side of the square are horse-drawn carriages for a romantic tour of the area.

And, of course, the Christmas Market (vánoční trh), the biggest and most spectacular of a dozen or so markets all over Prague, is a December visitor must-see. The centerpiece is the tall, decorated tree, donated by owners of private lands; it's an honor to have their tree chosen. Wooden huts around the square offer handcrafts and food, along with cups of Glühwein, a German mulled wine that's traditional at Christmas. Stages showcase village choirs that have traveled all the way to the capital city of Prague to perform; it's the highlight of their year!

At any time of day, and any season of the year, people are walking across the square with purpose on their way to work or taking care of civic chores. Not just for tourists, Old Town Square is still a crossroad for all kinds of business. If your tastes run to people-watching, stop for a coffee and pastry or a glass of wine in one of the cafes on the square and enjoy the show!

Staré Město (Old Town): Charles Bridge

So well-known that its image symbolizes Prague, Charles Bridge has connected Staré Město and Malá Strana since the fourteenth century, crossing the Vltava River as part of a major medieval trade route. Charles Bridge replaced an even older bridge, the Judith Bridge, which was built in 1172 and was destroyed in 1342 by the flooding Vltava river.

Under the auspices of King of Bohemia and Holy Roman Emperor Charles IV, construction of Charles Bridge began in 1357 and was completed in 1402. Peter Parler ("Petr Parléř" in Czech), the famous German-Czech architect responsible for St. Vitus Cathedral (Katedrála sv. Víta, Václava a Vojtěcha) in Hradčany, was in charge of the Charles Bridge project.

One feature you can't miss on Charles Bridge is the thirty statues of saints lining each side. From 1683 to 1938, these Gothic and Baroque-style statues of saints were carved to decorate the bridge.

The most famous statue is that of St. John of Nepomuk (Jan Nepomucký), installed in 1688–1689. Jan was a priest of the Church of Saint Giles (Kostel svatého Jiljí) in Prague's old Town. Legend has it that he served as confessor to the Queen, twenty-year-old Sophia of Bavaria. King Wenceslaus IV, suspicious of his young second wife's virtue, went to Jan to find out if she had been unfaithful.

When Jan refused to share the secrets of the confessional, the King arrested and tortured Jan. Despite these trials, the priest refused to reveal Queen Sophia's secrets. For this, his tongue was cut out, and he was tossed into the river and drowned. Later, when Wenceslaus left for his country estate, Jan was interred in St. Vitus Cathedral, a direct affront to the King. Jan of Nepomuk became a martyr for the faith in his defiance of the king, showing the power of the Church over that of royalty.

Located at the midpoint of Charles Bridge, the sculpture of Jan of Nepomuk features him in Roman vestments, holding a crucifix beneath a halo of five stars. Touching the plaque at its base is said to bring good luck and guarantee a return to Prague.

Walking across Charles Bridge is on so many bucket lists that it's practically mandated for any visitor to Prague. In the early morning and again in the evening, you can imagine yourself crossing the bridge six centuries ago, perhaps on a shopping trip to the markets of the Old Town (Staré Město) or going home to a tiny dwelling on the Lesser Town (Malá Strana).

Let your imagination run wild with scenes of the invading Swedish troops trying to cross Charles Bridge from Malá Strana to Staré Město in 1648, in the last battle of the Thirty Years' War. The Swedes were turned back by knights of the Order of Malta, the Burgher's Militia, and student troops led by

Catholic clergy, saving the city from destruction and looting.

Listen closely for the rushing waters of many floods that damaged the supporting piers over the centuries; the clopping of horses' hooves pulling wagons and trams over its stones; the rumble of an electric tram beginning in 1905; the burden of Russian tanks during the 1968 Soviet-led invasion of Prague; and millions of footsteps by visitors, tourists, and Prague-dwellers over more than six hundred years.

The bridge still stands, in spite of all that man and nature have done to it. I [Sara] can never get enough of this bridge, with its looming towers at either end, joining the spiritual and political power of Hradčany with the economic and educational energy of the Old and New Towns.

Charles Bridge is more than a pretty way to cross a river; it is a testament to the pride and tenacity of the citizens of Prague over many centuries of development. Take a photo of yourself on the bridge in happy, peaceful times, but remember the labor and sacrifice of thousands of people to build and defend this symbol of Prague.

After visiting Staré Město (Old Town) with its heavy freight of history and commerce, you can travel forward in time to Nové Město, the creation of Holy Roman Emperor and Bohemian King Charles IV in the fourteenth century. Nové Město translates as "New Town," and even though it's hardly new anymore, Nové Město still has a fresh and energetic spirit. The next chapter will give you a quick tour of both historical and modern Nové Město.

CHAPTER SIX: NOVÉ MĚSTO (NEW TOWN)

Defenestrations, horse markets and the Bohemian Crown Jewels! These are among the colorful stories of Nové Město over the six centuries that it has functioned as a showcase for both royal power and daily trade.

Just to get our terms straight, "New Town," founded by Charles IV in 1348, is not exactly new. It's only in contrast to Old Town that we can call this fourteenth-century urban expansion "new."

It's not hard to imagine why, in 1348, Holy Roman Emperor and Bohemian King Charles IV set out to build a brand-new district of Prague. The Old Town, charming as its narrow, winding cobbled streets were, was just about full. There were no large open spaces left within the city walls for ambitious projects such as new squares and markets, hospitals, churches, palaces, gardens, residential buildings, commercial shops, and small factories.

Malá Strana and Hradčany were not practical places for expansion, as they were hilly and already built up with the villas and palaces of the aristocracy, as well as craft workshops. The most practical solution was to design a brand-new, easy-to-maneuver grid of streets with spacious squares and plenty of room for new buildings. And this is what King Charles IV did!

Nové Město (New Town): finding your way around the district

When we lived in Prague from 2010-2013, we were in Nové Město at least once a day, it seemed. For everyday shopping, a quick meal at a café, and catching public transportation, New Town was our dependable neighborhood to conduct the practicalities of living in a big city.

Close to our home in Vinohrady, easily accessible on foot or by tram, the New Town is far enough from the tourist sites of Hradčany and the Old Town to have affordable rents. Interesting local shops and restaurants at reasonable prices make the New Town a welcome break from the crowds and high prices of the tourist-popular parts of Prague.

Tram 22, Prague's "tourist tram" that takes you from one side of the Vltava River to the other and hits all the high spots of Prague's tourist sites, goes right through Karlovo náměstí in the New Town. There's also a Metro station there.

We could board Tram 22 on Francouzská street in Vinohrady and be at Karlovo náměstí in minutes. If we stayed on, the tram turned north there and took us past the National Theatre and across the river with a perfect fairy-tale view of Hradčany on a hilltop.

New Town is laid out rationally, with long boulevards, geometric squares, and shorter cross streets. This logical plan makes it easy to find an address, though bear in mind the Prague system of posting street names and assigning street numbers.

Street signs are quite pretty, usually red with white letters, and are not on posts—they are attached to buildings, most often at intersections. By the way, the Czech word for street is ulice, as in Ječná ulice (Barley Street).

The street address is indicated by two signs, one blue and one red. The red signs were ordered by

Maria Teresa, Holy Roman Emperess, around 1770. They are in order from that date but don't reflect later, new buildings. In 1860, another system was set alongside the red signs: blue signs that included new buildings.

This system is confusing, but the way Czechs make it work is like this: addresses have two numbers, with the blue one being the mailing address. So you will find addresses like this: 426/35. The blue number is thirty-five and is typically the one you use to find the address on the street.

Now that you have a general idea of the layout of the New Town, you may want to take a few minutes to read about Charles IV's vision and how New Town has shaped Prague over the centuries.

Nové Město (New Town): the vision of Charles IV

Understanding a bit of history makes you grateful to Charles IV for having the forcsight and energy to analyze the needs of the growing city of Prague.

In March 1348, Charles IV issued the founding charter of Nové Město, the New Town of Prague, which established self-government for the town and assured that the rights and freedoms of the citizens of New Town would be the same as the citizens of Old Town.

On that March day in 1348, Charles IV issued another list, in which he liberated all the new settlers of Nové Město, including Jews, for twelve years from paying all tolls and taxes. This list also specifically designated the crafts to move to the established city within one year.

These craftspeople included confectioners, brewers, and blacksmiths. Many of the settlers in New Town were Czech tradesmen rather than the German merchants who dominated the older parts of Prague, giving the district a down-to-earth, workaday flavor.

Charles IV's anchor sites in Nové Město are three generously-sized public squares: the Horse Market - today's Wenceslas Square (Václavské náměstí), the Cattle Market - today's Karlovo náměstí (Charles Square), and the Hay Market - today's Senovážné Square.

Branching off from the squares, long, straight streets and boulevards were built, with smaller streets crossing at right angles in a rational grid plan. This plan produced much-improved transportation of goods and people, ensuring the rapid growth of Nové Město.

Nové Město (New Town): Karlovo náměstí (Charles Square)

Surrounded by banks, sidewalk cafes, coffee houses, and the Charles University medical offices, Karlovo náměstí is a good anchor point for a tour of Nové Město.

Here's an excerpt from Sara's book, *Prague for Beginners*, in which the narrator describes Charles Square:

> Karlovo náměstí, Charles Square, is bisected by a very busy street that crosses the river to Smíchov, so it's hard to get the full effect of its size. It's been a cattle market, a fish market, and a parade ground where Charles IV would display the crown jewels and his collection of holy relics on Easter.
>
> Now, both sides are parks, but the side we're on is less busy than the other and is laid out in walking paths among big old chestnut trees.

It's greening up nicely, giving the feeling of being out in the country somewhere, in spite of the cars whizzing by and the endless crowds of people. Some of them are tourists venturing away from the Old Town to see Charles IV's creation, the New Town he laid out in 1348, with big squares surrounded by gridded streets. Here he put his New Town Hall, which is no longer new. It's a nice-looking building, city-owned and closed to the public.

Charles Square is a true city square, the kind of place that people walk through on the way to somewhere else. It also has quiet benches tucked away under the canopy of trees, pretty statues, and flowerbeds, tempting the walkers to enjoy a moment of relaxation.

You can see people of all ages, from all over the world, in Charles Square. A quick lunch on a sidewalk café can be a chance to soak up the sunshine on a bright day, or you can sit for a few minutes inside a coffee shop, just enjoying the passing scene.

Nové Město (New Town): New Town Hall (Novoměstská radnice)

It's not every city that can boast not just one, but two, political defenestrations and even got its own word invented.

Defenestration ("de, down from" and "fenestra, window or opening") is the act of throwing someone or something out of a window. The word is not found in original Latin. It's a neologism, a new word, made up for a specific occasion in 1618, when Protestant leaders threw two Catholic councilmen out of a window in Prague Castle.

By extension, the word is applied to the First Defenestration, which happened in 1419 in the New Town Hall. A Hussite (Protestant) mob marched in to demand the release of Hussite believers imprisoned there. When the Catholic officials refused, the mob threw nine officials out the window: a judge, seven councilmen, and the chief magistrate. Under the window were spears pointed upward by Hussite zealots, to make sure that all nine died.

This act that ignited the Hussite Wars (1419–1434), in which Protestant Hussites battled Catholics for control of Bohemia. To squash this revolt, in 1420 Pope Martin V ordered a crusade against "Wycliffites, Hussites and all other heretics in Bohemia," in which the armies of the Holy Roman Empire were unsuccessful in ousting the Hussites.

The history of the Hussites is too long and complicated to detail in this book. Both *Prague in Black and Gold* by Peter Demetz and *The Czechs and the Lands of the Bohemian Crown* by Hugh Agnew give a full account of how the Hussite movement shaped Bohemia and modern-day Czech Republic.

Nové Město (New Town): Wenceslas Square (Václavské náměstí)

Many Czechs would say that the heart of Prague is Václavské náměstí, especially the busy foot of the square at Můstek, a metro stop named for the "little bridge" across the Old Town moat in the Middle Ages.

This long square, the former horse market, is the traditional gathering place for civic events, such as demonstrations during the peaceful Velvet Revolution in November 1989, when the Communist government exited Czechoslovakia, and the country was suddenly free for the first time since 1948.

Here's an excerpt from Sara's novel, *Prague for Beginners*, in which the narrator describes Wenceslas Square:

If Wenceslas Square could talk, it would have a lot to say. As the silent eyes of a nation, the square has witnessed a great deal of Czech history—from its humble beginnings as a horse market in medieval times to a giant Mass held during the revolutionary upheavals of 1848 to the celebration of the creation of the new Czechoslovak Republic in 1918 to the peaceful Velvet Revolution of 1989 to its present-day status as the meeting place of choice for Czech citizens and tourists alike.

Wenceslas Square is a contradiction of styles: beautiful Art Nouveau edifices and baroque architecture are juxtaposed with faceless Soviet-era department stores.

Wenceslas Square has become a monument to capitalism and is encased by upmarket hotels, fast food outlets, nightclubs, foreign exchange offices, and international clothing shops, restaurants, and bars.

At the top end of the square is the National Museum, a dignified neo-Renaissance building that looks down the whole square. It is the oldest and largest museum in the Czech Republic.

A few minutes' walk from the National Museum is the Prague State Opera, with performances of opera and ballet which cater to local and tourist clientele. In the blocks around the square, residential neighborhoods mix with cafés and shops with regional arts.

Wenceslas Square (Václavské náměstí), with its benches and pleasant, open skies, is a traditional meeting place for all kinds of people, from tourists to locals. Many city tour buses depart from the square, and it is flanked by two metro stations, Můstek and Museum. You may find yourself more than once in Wenceslas Square.

Nové Město (New Town): Náměstí Republiky

Náměstí Republiky has been part of the city walls, a royal court, part of the king's coronation route, and a civic gathering place. The oldest part is the Powder Tower, Prašná brána, built in 1475 and redone in high Gothic in the 1800s. It's the traditional divide between the Old Town and the New Town.

If you are entering from Celetná street in the Old Town, turn left after you walk under the archway of the Powder Tower, and you enter Náměstí Republiky, a large, open square fronted with buildings from different eras, reflecting its age. It's on the site of an old moat and was once home to Czech kings, such as Václav IV (in the fourteenth century) and Vladislav Jagellonský (in the fifteenth century).

Here's an excerpt from Sara's book, *Prague for Beginners*, in which the narrator describes Náměstí Republiky:

> Then comes the Municipal House, Obecní dům, an art Nouveau explosion built over the remains of the old royal court between 1905-1911, as the Habsburg Empire was breathing its last breath.
>
> It's a remarkable building, curved and straight at the same time with a huge allegorical mural over the front doors; in 1918, the declaration of Czechoslovak nationhood was read from its balcony. Next to it stands Kotva, another Brutalist 1970s Communist work of art built as a department store.
>
> The big open square has tram tracks hidden in the cobblestones of the square's pavement; I have nearly gotten run over by trams, which have the right-of-way over everything. On the other side is a plain church that is ornately Baroque inside, and a new, shiny glass mall built on the site of an old army barracks.

With its central location just a few blocks from the Old Town Square, its convenient transportation, its easy shopping, and its access to the Municipal House (the site of concerts and two restaurants), Náměstí Republiky has elements of historic Prague and of the modern, busy city as well.

It could be, though, that you are ready for a break. The next chapter describes green spaces in Prague: parks, gardens, and pathways that offer clean air, a respite from sightseeing, and glimpses of daily life in the city.

CHAPTER SEVEN: GREEN SPACES OF PRAGUE

There is one wonderful thing about Prague, frequently missed by many visitors, especially those who are eager to see as many iconic landmarks in the city as possible in a short period of time. That thing can be best described as its many superb green spaces, including picturesque gardens, numerous parks, and nature preserves where you can find serene, quiet places in the midst of the bustling city to relax and enjoy nature.

We have chosen a few outstanding places that we often visit ourselves, but a little exploration will reveal to you dozens of such glorious gardens and parks all over the city of Prague.

An easy walk from the Old Town, across Charles Bridge over the Vltava River, is Prague's Malá Strana (Lesser Town), and not far from the Lesser Town Square is Vrtba Garden (Vrtbovská zahrada), where we will start our visit. This should result in getting an entirely new impression of the city.

We'll then proceed to visit Wallenstein Garden under Hradčany Castle and several other "must-see" green spaces including Stromovka Park, Petřín Hill, Prague's Botanical Gardens, Břevnov Monastery (Břevnovský klášter), Hvězda, and Průhonice Castle Park. All of these refreshing places offer diverse natural beauty, tranquil retreats, and delightful views.

Green Spaces of Prague: Vrtba Garden (Vrtbovská zahrada)

Vrtba Garden is a Baroque garden whose modest entrance is almost hidden on busy Karmelitská Street (number 25), near Malostranské Náměstí. Once inside the garden, you can appreciate its quiet charm.

It's a unique complex of precisely-designed flower beds and white staircases adorned with statues of ancient Roman gods and goddesses, and is known for its serenity, scenic views, and historical setting. The garden features lookout areas from which you have spectacular views of Prague Castle (Hradčany) and of the city of Prague on both sides of the Vltava River.

Together with three other Baroque gardens (Vratislav, Schönborn and Lobkowicz), the Vrtba Garden is situated on the slope of Petřín Hill. Vrtba is an Italian-style Baroque terrace-garden and was built for Jan Josef, Count of Vrtba, the Highest Burgrave of Prague Castle, near Vrtba Palace in 1715 - 1720.

The garden is usually not crowded and has an air of peacefulness and grace that makes its flower beds and greenery an oasis of calm in the busy Lesser Town streets. The next green space we'll explore is nearby Wallenstein Garden, about 10 minutes of easy walking from Malostranské náměstí.

Green Spaces of Prague: The Wallenstein (or Waldstein) Garden (Valdštejnská zahrada)

Wallenstein Garden gives us another well-preserved example of Baroque design in Prague, with its statues, sculptures, and dramatic views of Hradčany castle. The garden was created in parallel with the construction of Wallenstein Palace from 1623 to 1629.

Albrecht von Wallenstein was a colorful character. He led armies of the Holy Roman Empire against the Protestant nobles of Bohemia during the Thirty Years' War (1618-1648), gaining fame at the battle of White Mountain in 1620.

Emperor Ferdinand II appointed Wallenstein as Duke of Freidland, as well as Supreme Commander and Admiral of the Baltic Seas, but later dismissed Wallenstein, suspicious of his ambition. On the Emperor's orders Wallenstein was assassinated in

1634, amid accusations of high treason. He had just a few years to enjoy his palace and garden.

Wallenstein Garden is rarely visited by tourists, as it's not easy to find. You walk about halfway down Letenská street in Malá Strana, looking for a small, wooden door in the tall stucco wall. This door leads into the garden. If you hear the screaming of peacocks behind the wall, you are in the right place!

Fountains, statues, a man-made grotto, a caged owl refuge, and those roaming peacocks make it hard to remember that you're next to a big Metro station in the busiest part of Malá Strana.

Wallenstein Garden is a peaceful retreat from crowds and offers a glimpse into historical landscape design, giving you an idea of how a wealthy nobleman passed his time in his city villa.

The building is accessible when the Senate is not in session. You can visit the website to get a schedule. There are rules in the garden: don't touch or feed the animals, don't gather peacock feathers for souvenirs, and (not surprisingly) no dogs allowed.

Green Spaces of Prague: Petřín Hill

Interspersed among the woods and grassy spaces of Petřín Hill are enough varied sites to entertain a family for an afternoon. Enjoy the panoramic city views from the Petřín Lookout Tower (a mini-Eiffel Tower), accessible by a funicular railway.

Walk the Mirror Maze (Zrcadlové bludiště na Petříně), good fun for both children and adults. From the outside, the building resembles a small castle, and inside is a hall made of mirrors. A diorama of the battle of the Praguers against the Swedes at the Charles Bridge in 1648 gives a bit of history, and the "hall of laughter" has warped and twisted mirrors that will change your appearance in crazy ways.

Outside, there is a Rose Garden on the top of the hill. Very close to the Rose Garden is an astronomical observatory. As a child, I [Jarda] often visited this observatory with my close relative, who was an astronomer. The whole experience of visiting Petřín Hill was a highlight of my childhood.

You can also visit the Seminary Garden (which contains thousands of fruit trees of a great variety), an herbal garden, the Kinsky Garden, and the Lobkowicz Gardens. Historical features like the medieval Hunger Wall and quarry pits give you an idea of the age and significance of Petřín Hill.

The hill offers many hiking trails and paths for biking, and the views of Prague are worth your time.

From Petřín Hill it's convenient to move to our next locations, Břevnov Monastery on Bělohorská ulice (street) and Obora Hvězda (Star Game Reserve) located in Prague-Liboc.

Green Spaces of Prague: Břevnov Monastery (Břevnovský klášter)

Břevnov Monastery was founded in 998 AD by Boleslav II and Bishop Adalbert, making it the oldest Bohemian monastery in the Benedictine tradition. It's surrounded by well-maintained, quiet gardens, a cloister wall, and an orangery. All green spaces of this attractive monastery complex are open to the general public.

Břevnov Monastery's current appearance, dating back to 1708-1745, is an example of High Baroque style. The monastery is known for its brewery, the existence of which was documented as early as in the thirteenth century. You can enjoy a sample of the brewer's art in the Cloister Tavern (Klášterní šenk) and spend the night in the Hotel Adalbert (former monastery quarters, remodeled with an eye to preserving the original features), built by M.

Reiner between 1668 and 1674 and modified by K. I. Dientzenhofer (1735).

The quiet, calming green spaces of Břevnov Monastery are located only a short distance from a spacious nature reserve, Obora Hvězda.

Green Spaces of Prague: Obora Hvězda (Star Game Reserve)

Founded in the sixteenth century, this large, hilly, wooded park with many hiking trails and creeks features a summer palace in the shape of a six-pointed star (Hvězda in Czech). The park offers pleasant areas for hiking in nature or for walking your dog.

The unique, star-shaped Letohrádek Hvězda is a Renaissance summer palace built in 1555 for Archduke Ferdinand II. Used in those days for entertaining and as a hunting lodge, Hvězda now houses museums and galleries.

Our next green space location, the Royal Game Reserve Stromovka (Královská obora Stromovka), which is located in the Bubeneč district of Prague, has a very different character from Obora Hvězda.

Green Spaces of Prague: Royal Game Reserve Stromovka (Královská obora Stromovka)

As its title suggests, Stromovka is a former royal hunting preserve. In 1804 it was transformed into a publicly accessible park maintained in the style of an English park, known for its vast green spaces, ponds, trails, and a summer house in Neo Gothic style.

Stromovka was established in the thirteenth century as a game reserve for the pleasure of the king. Later, Emperor Rudolph II, during his reign in the sixteenth century, had rare trees planted there near the Vltava River and several lakes created.

As the city of Prague developed around it, Stromovka was opened to public use. Playgrounds, roads, and trails were added, giving visitors places to walk, picnic, cycle, and relax. Restaurants and a planetarium offer more opportunities for people to spend the afternoon in the park.

The whole reserve could be seen as Prague's Central Park. It's located close to Chateau Troja (Trojský zámek), the Prague Zoo, and Prague Botanical Garden in Troja.

To get from Stromovka Park to the Prague Zoo, you can walk across the Troja Bridge, take a scenic boat cruise from central Prague (from Rašín Embankment, for example) right to the zoo's island, or use public transport.

Green Spaces of Prague: Prague Botanical Garden in Troja (Pražská botanická zahrada hlavního města Prahy)

The Prague Botanical Garden, located near Chateau Troja (Trojský zámek) and the Prague Zoo, offers a relaxing atmosphere, inviting exploration and fun in the midst of thousands of species of trees and flowers.

Established in 1968, the Prague Botanical Garden is dedicated to plant conservation, biodiversity research, and educating the public on ecology and nature. Notable exhibits include the Japanese Garden and Fata Morgana Greenhouse.

The garden features the historic St. Claire's Vineyard, established during the reign of Wenceslas II (1278-1305). Charles IV issued a decree about vineyard establishment and made all suitable south-facing slopes within three miles of Prague mandatorily planted with grapevine, ensuring that this vineyard would be continuously cultivated.

The garden offers a tropical rainforest environment, complete with waterfalls and a wide variety of orchids. It provides for visitors an example of a well-managed green space in a quiet setting, and it offers an escape from Prague's busy life.

Last but not least, we recommend visiting Průhonice Chateau and Botanical Park, about a twenty minute drive from Prague's center.

Green Spaces of Prague: Průhonice Chateau and Botanical Park (Průhonický park)

This spacious park is a Czech National Historic Landmark and is listed as a UNESCO World Heritage Site. Průhonice Park is home to more than a thousand different kinds of plants including rhododendrons and a unique Alpine Garden (Alpium), as well as streams, ponds, and more than twenty-five kilometers of pathways.

There are also a quaint chateau/castle complex and a church dating back to the twelfth century. It's located about fifteen km from Prague's city center and accessible by public bus or taxi.

Here's an excerpt from Sara's novel, *Prague for Beginners*:

> Průhonice is a former village just outside Prague, now part of the city, with an enormous park, in the sense that royalty has a park: an immense

family property thick with meticulously-tended trees, shrubs, flower beds, streams, and secluded places to sit and admire the view.

The brochure I got the last time I visited says that Průhonice Park is currently owned by the State and is the headquarters of the Institute of Botany of the Academy of Sciences of the Czech Republic, a grand-sounding organization whose headquarters consists of a few offices in the old vicarage. They've been there since 1962.

I buy a ticket and enter the gates. Stretching in front of me are trees and shrubs, cut by a winding path that branches left and right. I go left to look at the small, old Church of the Holy Virgin Birth, which I know is open only for Mass on Sunday morning; maybe I'll catch a glimpse if someone is cleaning it. No, not today. I pass the Institute offices and an open set of gates, then stop to admire the view of the castle in front of me.

My brochure states that the present castle, like nearly every old building in the Czech Republic, is not at all what it looked like originally. The first records date to 1270, and historians imagine it was a small fortress, plainly built, with a tower to use as a retreat in case of attack.

The fortress was reconstructed in Renaissance style in the sixteenth century and devastated in the Thirty Years' War, the terribly destructive religious/political war from 1618-1648 between peasants and royalty, Protestants and Catholics; nearly one-third of the people living in Bohemia died in this war.

It was rebuilt, briefly owned by Jesuits, destroyed again by war in the eighteenth century, rebuilt again, deserted, used as a farm, bought by a Portuguese nobleman who married a Czech countess, and once again rebuilt in 1885. The Count's architects turned the building, a modest manor house at the time, into a fantasy castle with spires, cupolas, domes, statues, wrought-iron balconies, and other neo-Renaissance, Gothic, and Romantic details.

No one is in sight, so I take pictures and amuse myself by sketching and walking slowly around the front courtyard. Then I enter one of the tunnels that leads to the inner courtyard, where the view of the gardens opens up before me. I stand and examine below me the dramatic landscape that the Count created with his team of landscape architects.

To the left is a long "mountain" pond made by damming the brook, surrounded by towering evergreens and huge rocks. A winding path to the right goes around another pond, then opens out to acres of gently rolling hills, rocky outcrops, planted flowerbeds, wildflowers, streams, ponds, and walking paths.

Spring is advancing with determination. The trees are budding, leafing out, and beginning to blossom according to their individual patterns. Most of the shrubs are fully green. Beds of hyacinths and daffodils are filled with flowers pushing up, green leaves unfurling as they rise. The ground is moist, giving out a rich smell of life after the long, snowy winter.

I find one of my favorite seats, a concrete bench with wooden arms next to a small round pond. The day is warming up, and I take off my sweater. I sit in the sun and fall into a pleasant doze.

A snapping noise wakes me. Near the pond is a deer, nibbling on the new grass. He doesn't see or smell me. For the next few minutes, I watch him move at a leisurely pace, quite at one with his surroundings. He looks up sharply, perhaps getting a whiff of me, swings his head in my direction, then turns and ambles off into the woods. I pick up my notebook and sketch the deer. I add the pond and trees, date and sign it. Time to head back to Prague.

The City of Prague and its surroundings boast many diverse green spaces ranging from vast natural reserves like Hvězda to manicured Baroque Gardens such as the Vrtba Gardens and large parks such as Petřín Gardens or Průhonice Botanical Gardens. Such abundant green spaces offer visitors an escape from urban life and contribute to Prague's reputation as a "Green City."

CHAPTER EIGHT: QUIET SANCTUARIES IN THE BIG CITY

It's not hard to find a quiet place in Prague to take a moment of peace. The tourist areas are crowded in the summer, but just a few steps away from the crowds are cool, serene buildings; tiny, cobbled squares; and miniature gardens where you can catch your breath.

Many of these places have a religious origin. As in all European capital cities, there's a huge diversity of cathedrals, neighborhood churches, monasteries, cemeteries, pilgrimage sites, and chapels. As well, in Prague, the millennium-long Jewish community has built synagogues and cemeteries.

Here we have gathered a few of our favorite places to relax and renew ourselves. Most of these places fit into a larger historical context, and if you are interested in learning more about the history of Prague, we can suggest three books:

Hugh Agnew, *The Czechs and the Lands of the Bohemian Crown.* Hoover Institution Press, 2013.

Peter Demetz, *Prague in Black and Gold: Scenes in the Life of a European City.* Hill & Wang, New York, 1997.

Sara Tusek, *Prague for Beginners: Finding Myself in Prague.* International Leadership Institute Publications, Lake Mary, FL, 2017.

Quiet Sanctuaries in the Big City: St. Nicholas Church (Chrám sv. Mikuláše) in Staroměstské náměstí

Tucked away in a quiet corner of the Old Town Square (Staroměstské náměstí), St, Nicholas Church was built from 1732-1737 according to plans by Kilián Ignaz Dientzenhofer, Prague's favorite Baroque architect. Not as grand as the St. Nicholas Church in Malá Strana, this church has a human scale and soothing atmosphere. The church hosts concerts on a regular basis.

I [Sara] once attended a performance of Mozart's *Requiem* in this church and was moved to tears by the harmony of the solemn, stately music and the serene interior of the church. I had sung this piece when I lived in Sewanee, in Latin, and the Czech choir also performed in Latin, so I could lose myself in the words and music.

Behind the church is Franz Kafka Square, one of the smallest and newest squares in the city, named after the writer, who was born right here. Kafka spent most of his early life in and around Old Town Square, and his Prague roots are found in his writings. *Metamorphosis* (1915) is probably Franz Kafka's most famous and influential work.

Quiet Sanctuaries in the Big City: Břevnov Monastery (Břevnovský Klášter)

This monastery complex is also covered in Chapter Seven, Green Spaces of Prague. For a more personal touch, here is an excerpt from Sara's *Prague for Beginners*:

> At Břevnovský klášter I get off the tram and head for the walled compound, hoping to find the kostel svaté Markéty, St. Margaret's Church, open. As I pass through the tunnel into the cloister complex, I note the relative warmth of the air and decide I can sit outside if need be.
>
> I am behind Břevnovský klášter, where someone long ago nailed a series of carved wooden figures to the trees; these fourteen stations of the cross commemorate the journey of Jesus to the cross on the day he was crucified. The ground flattens further down, as I walk past the Bishops' Residence.

The monastery was established in 992 by Vojtěch, the Bishop of Prague, and the Bohemian Prince Boleslav II, making Břevnov Monastery the oldest Benedictine monastery in the Czech Republic. I've read all I can find on this monastery and quizzed Marek; it's become my favorite place in Prague, a spiritual retreat with a history of saintly devotion and wicked violence so intertwined they can't be separated.

It seems that no corner of Prague is all good or all bad; like humans themselves, the city has places of high spiritual energy right next to more sinister spots where greed and the lust for power have caused misery and destruction.

What makes Prague's quiet places all the more precious to me [Sara] is the message of hope (sometimes 'hope against hope") and restoration that is evident in every one of these quiet places.

The U.S. is a young country, and we have yet to see how our ongoing struggles between good and bad will play out. Prague gives me hope that time, good intentions, and perseverance can overcome all manner of catastrophes.

Quiet Sanctuaries in the Big City: Synagogues and Cemeteries

Prague is graced with a great diversity of religious places, including synagogues and cemeteries for its Jewish community.

Josefov is the neighborhood where most of the treasures of traditional Jewish life in Prague will be found. We have talked about the history of Josefov in Chapter Five: Staré Město (Old Town), so here we will focus on the Old-New Synagogue and the Old Jewish Cemetery.

You have two choices in Josefov: do your own walking tour, perhaps with a map or podcast, or visit the Jewish Museum of Prague for detailed information and tickets to the various sites (Maisel, Spanish, Klaus, Pinkas, and Old-New synagogues; Ceremonial Hall; Old Jewish Cemetery and Robert Guttmann Gallery).

Either way, you can get a sense of the age and human history in Josefov. A city within a city, the Jewish heritage of the walled ghetto, the relative freedom granted by Josef II, and the urban renewal demolition of the area in the 1880s can be seen in the winding streets and varied architecture.

Quiet Sanctuaries in the Big City: Old-New Synagogue

The main synagogue of the Prague Jewish community for more than seven hundred years, the Old-New Synagogue is the oldest site of Prague's Jewish Town and the oldest still-standing synagogue in Europe.

Called the New or Great Shul when it was completed, it took on the name of Old-New after other synagogues were established in the late sixteenth century. The construction of these new synagogues corresponded to the rising prosperity of Josefov, due in large part to the generosity of Mordechai Maisel, wealthy mayor and philanthropist.

As with most old buildings in Prague, numerous legends and tales are tied to the Old-New synagogue. According to one legend, the attic of the synagogue is the home to the remains of the Golem, the artificial creature made of clay that was animated by Judah Loew ben Bezalel, Talmudic scholar, Jewish mystic, mathematician, astronomer, and philosopher, who, for most of his life, served as rabbi in Moravia and Prague.

In medieval Jewish mysticism, a golem is shaped out of an inanimate material and brought to life by magic. Golems are created for specific purposes, to help their creator. But often, in golem legends, the creature becomes uncontrollable.

Rabbi Lowe, according to legend, formed his golem out of clay from the Vltava River. The rabbi placed a *shem* (a parchment with a holy name) in its mouth to bring it to "life." But any good intentions the rabbi may have had were shattered by the violent and destructive nature of the golem.

Before long, the rabbi removed the *shem* and the golem was just a lump of clay again. The golem is said to be in the attic of the Old-New Synagogue, perhaps biding its time till it becomes animated again.

Quiet Sanctuaries in the Big City: Old Jewish Cemetery

Josefov's Old Jewish Cemetery is one of Europe's oldest surviving Jewish burial grounds. It was, until the opening of the Žižkov Jewish Cemetery in 1680, the only place for Jewish burials in and around Prague.

Note: you can read more about the Žižkov Jewish Cemetery in "Chapter Two: Fun Times in Žižkov."

In use between 1439 and 1787, the Old Jewish Cemetery contains more than twelve thousand tombstones. Because of the ghetto's limited space and Jewish burial customs, which prohibit the disturbance of graves, new burials were stacked on top of previous ones. According to some researchers, the burials are up to ten layers deep.

Over the centuries, the ground has subsided, causing the tombstones to tilt at different angles.

The crowded and tilted tombstones give the cemetery a melancholy feeling, especially as the cemetery is quite small and completely shaded with big, old trees. You can almost imagine you are in an ancient rural cemetery, absorbing the quiet and peace in this burial place.

Quiet Sanctuaries in the Big City: The Church of St. Giles (Kostel sv. Jiljí)

St. Giles (sv. Jiljí) is not one of the best-known of the Catholic saints. How a gorgeous Baroque church in Prague was dedicated to him is a bit of mystery. Here's the story:

Born in the first half of the seventh century in southeastern France, St. Giles built a monastery that became a popular way station for pilgrims making their way to Compostela in Spain and to the Holy Land.

In Germany, St. Giles was included among the Fourteen Holy Helpers, saints to whom people prayed for recovery from disease and for strength at the hour of death. St. Giles became known as the patron of the poor and the disabled.

The Order of Brothers of the German House of Saint Mary in Jerusalem (commonly known as the

Teutonic Knights) had formed in 1191 to aid the journey of pilgrims travelling from Europe to Jerusalem; they are associated with creating hospitals on the route. In 1238, the Knights built the Romanesque-style St. Giles Church, perhaps calling on St. Giles to aid travelers and pilgrims in the tradition of their order.

In 1420, during the Hussite Wars, St. Giles was taken over by Protestant Hussites. After the Battle of White Mountain in 1620, when the Catholic Habsburgs defeated the Protestant Czech nobles, the church was donated in 1625 to the Dominican order. They restored and rebuilt the church in Baroque style, as well as adding a monastery.

As was the fate of many churches in Prague during communist rule, St. Giles was closed in 1950, and the monks were forced into labor camps. In 1990 St. Giles was returned to the Catholic church and revitalized, undoing the damage of forty years of neglect.

A young Polish priest has made St. Giles church very popular among Prague's young generation since 2007, and the church is known for active and vigorous ongoing activities designed to help handicapped people.

When I [Jarda] am in Prague, I often visit this church on sunny days because the rays of afternoon sunshine that shine through the church's windows create an unforgettable and powerful effect, resulting in a deep spiritual experience of marveling about the wonders of God's creation.

Quiet Sanctuaries in the Big City: Olšanské hřbitovy (the Olšany cemeteries)

Olšanské hřbitovy (the Olšany cemeteries) are Prague's largest burial complex and the most extensive graveyard in the Czech Republic. Covering over fifty hectares, comprising twelve individual cemeteries, and resembling an extensive urban park, the rectangular site is divided into two sections by Jana Želivského Street.

The first cemetery was created in 1680 on the site of the village of Olšany after the plague epidemic of 1679. In 1786, Emperor Josef II banned all burials within the city walls on the grounds of hygiene, and Olšany cemetery became Prague's main burial ground. In 1886, a new Jewish cemetery and synagogue were added to the first cemetery, which was subsequently enlarged several times.

To walk through Olšany is to be transported to another era. Especially in the older parts, gently-decaying tombs and monuments under thick, green foliage of trees, shrubs, and grave plantings create an atmosphere of isolation from the surrounding city of Prague.

Impressive sculptures by leading Czech artists such as Ignác Platzer, Josef Zítek, J. V. Myslbek, Františck Bílck, and Olbram Zoubek add to the dignity and solemnity of the cemeteries. Walkways can be straight or winding, making it easy to get a bit lost without a map, but getting lost can be the best part of visiting Olšany, allowing you to absorb the past glories of Prague.

Since 1680, more than two million people have been laid to rest in the cemeteries—some buried, some entombed, and some cremated. The walls around the cemeteries are lined with small glass-fronted boxes containing urns of ashes.

Many prominent Czech figures are found in Olšany, including student Jan Palach (martyr), Klement Gottwald (politician), Božena Němcová (writer), Franz Kafka (writer), Viktor Dyk (writer), Karel

Kramář (politician), the son and granddaughters of President T. G. Masaryk, and theatre personalities Jan Werich and Jiří Voskovec.

A visit to Olšany is part of every visit we make to Prague, as Jarda's parents and other ancestors are buried there. Something about the calm dignity of Olšany makes each visit a special moment to give thanks for the past and look forward to the future.

Quiet Sanctuaries in the Big City: Church of Our Lady of the Snows (Panny Marie Sněžné)

Both Jarda and I [Sara] love this church. I've written about it in *Prague for Beginners:*

> My eyes light on the tall, white ship of a building, Kostel Panny Marie Sněžné (the church and monastery of Our Lady of the Snows), that dominates the skyline. Marek took me there once when I first moved to Prague. He told me that it is usually unlocked, so I decided to try it.
>
> To get there, I walk through the Františkánská zahrada, a neat, city-sized garden next to the church. The garden originally belonged to the Franciscans, who were given the church in 1607 by Rudolf II. During Communism, the garden was "liberated" from the clutches of the Roman Catholic Church and turned over to the Czechoslovak common people, the Proletariat,

who trashed it as an expression of their deep gratitude to the State.

After the Velvet Revolution of 1989, parts of the gardens were returned to the Franciscans, and the entire garden area was renovated. Now it's an unexpected pleasure, a pretty, rural garden with trellised roses, between the commercial Václavské náměstí and Jungmannovo náměstí.

Panny Marie Sněžné is very tall and odd-looking. Marek told me it was meant to be the second-biggest in Prague but never got finished, as the money ran out after this first part was built.

It was founded by the Carmelite order of monks, who were a mendicant order, meaning they were beggars forbidden by their own rules to own anything.

Building a church was far beyond their means, but Charles IV, who built churches all over Prague during his reign, wanted a church here. He donated the land and building materials; soon enough the east end of the church—the chancel, or presbytery, where the altar and choir stalls are located—was complete, but the rest of the church was never built.

As in most Gothic cathedrals, the chancel of Panny Marie Sněžné is housed in the semi-circular end of the building, with stained-glass windows and all kinds of finely-carved pillars and screens. This chancel also originally had an attached bell tower which was damaged in the Hussite Wars of the 15th century; it collapsed a century later.

The entire building crumbled into a ruin, and the Carmelites abandoned it. Rudolf II later gave it to the Franciscans to let them have a go at making it useful. They did and are still here after a few interregnums in the 20th century.

The door is unlocked, which is unusual for Prague; most churches can be entered only during services. The church interior is Baroque, but more restrained than the usual colorful riot of paintings and altars. It's empty, and I slip into a back pew.

Slipping into a back pew at Panny Marie Sněžné is always a pleasure for Jarda and me [Sara]. The light is dim; the church smells like stone and dust. The wooden pews are simple and not very comfortable, so there's little temptation to linger.

A quick moment of contemplation and a brief prayer is enough to refresh the mind and spirit. We highly recommend an interlude in Panny Marie Sněžné to brighten a busy day and renew a tired mind.

Quiet Sanctuaries in the Big City: The Church of St. Ignatius (Kostel sv. Ignáce)

The Church of St. Ignatius of Loyola on the southern edge of Charles Square was constructed between 1664 and 1671. It served as an important center for Jesuit education and Counter-Reformation activities until Emperor Josef II expelled the Jesuits from Bohemia in 1773, when their order was suppressed by the Catholic Church. The Jesuit College was repurposed as military barracks by the Emperor.

From Sara's novel, *Prague for Beginners*:

> A grandly ornate building, now grey from car exhaust and soot-stained with crumbling pillars, Kostel sv. Ignáce is one of dozens built around the city in the 1600s after the Austrians added Bohemia to their empire. It's as Catholic as can be, named for the founder of the Jesuit order of priests.

It's had the typical up-and-down history of Prague's Catholic churches: built in victory from 1665-1671, the church was run by Jesuits till 1773, when Austrian Emperor Josef II drove them out of Bohemia. In 1886, the Jesuits returned and ran the church this time until 1950, when the Communists drove them out. In 1991, they returned again and took back the neglected building.

I've imagined that it's beautiful inside, styled in the Rococo Baroque of cherubs, swirling plaster flowers and banners, elaborate pulpit, and many individual side altars with paintings and statues, but I've never been inside, as the doors have been locked when I've tried.

In truth, I [Sara] have only had glimpses of this church from the doorway. It is usually locked except during services and hours for confession, so out of respect I haven't entered as a tourist when it was open.

My fascination is with the exterior, which is somewhat dwarfed by the large buildings around

Charles Square. Traffic whizzes right past the church on Ječná ulice (street), while trams and a Metro stop load and unload crowds of people just a few feet away. Yet it maintains its authority in spite of the encroachments of the twenty-first century, its rather shabby walls standing firm. I like it.

Quiet Sanctuaries in the Big City: Vyšehrad

Vyšehrad ("upper castle") is a tenth-century settlement on the east bank of the Vltava River, across and upstream from Hradčany. Inside the walls are the Basilica of St. Peter and St. Paul and the Vyšehrad Cemetery, which is the resting place of prominent Czechs including Antonín Dvořák, Bedřich Smetana, Karel Čapek, and Alphonse Mucha.

Legend has it that Duke Krok founded Vyšehrad on a steep rock face above the Vltava river. Another legend states that Prince Křesomysl imprisoned the knight Horymír at Vyšehrad because he damaged silver mines, and Horymír jumped with his horse Šemík over the walls into the river.

From Sara's novel, *Prague for Beginners*:

> I take the Metro back toward the city center and on impulse get off at Vyšehrad, the "other castle."

Marek took me here once to show me the impressive national cemetery full of elaborate grave markers and decorated tombs where many of the most famous and accomplished Czech artists, composers, musicians, political figures, and writers are laid to rest.

Vyšehrad is the site of a tenth-century fort built on a tall, rocky hill that sits on the right bank of the Vltava. Legends about the founders of Bohemia living at Vyšehrad are interwoven with true stories of sieges and abandonments of the fortifications over the centuries.

In the eleventh century, Vratislav, a Bohemian prince, made Vyšehrad his official court and built a royal residence and church there; after his death, it fell into a state of disrepair. In the fourteenth century, Charles IV, the emperor who built Prague's New Town, rebuilt Vyšehrad to a respectable state, but the Hussite armies of the fifteenth century ransacked it.

In the same century, during a political power struggle, the troops of Czech nobleman Jiří z

Poděbrad, who later became King George of Poděbrady, the only Protestant Bohemian king, attacked Vyšehrad again, leaving it a total ruin.

The Habsburg monarchy, those Austrian Catholics who put a layer of fanciful Baroque decoration wherever they could in Prague to show the rebellious Bohemians who was in charge, rebuilt Vyšehrad in the seventeenth century and made it an army training center. This is the rough equivalent of having Canada invade the US and take over the government, then making Arlington National Cemetery into a campground for Canadian troops. A desecration.

Since then, Vyšehrad has been maintained and periodically modernized. Now it's a public park and nice place to stroll on a weekday, when there are no tourists or Czech family groups. You can walk to the ramparts, the old city walls, and look down over the Vltava River. To the south are the suburbs of Prague; to the north is Hradčany, with the two towers of St. Vitus Cathedral poking into the sky.

Today I am at the ramparts looking downstream at Hradčany. The grey skies seem low and oppressive. There are bits of fog all around me; I guess the river and the hill produce local fogs that come and go.

It's romantic and atmospheric; I can imagine myself a fourteenth-century soldier on guard duty for Prince Vratislav, wary of would-be assassins scaling the rock from the river below. It's also easy to imagine myself the Prince's daughter, in love with my tutor, a poor French student who is meeting me in the silent, foggy afternoon against my father's wishes.

I am the only human in sight, with a gentle snowstorm enveloping me, with the Basilica of St. Peter and St. Paul, a tall stone Gothic church, in front of me, stone figures of ancient legendary figures next to me, and the cloistered cemetery just past the church. I feel that I could easily disappear without a trace.

I leave by the path that takes me past St. Martin's Rotunda, an eleventh- century round stone building said to be the oldest unchanged building in Prague. It's only open from time to time for services, which makes it doubly enchanting and mysterious. In the gentle snow and dim light, I feel I could be a postulant hurrying to Mass, though there are no convents here, and why would a lone postulant be traipsing around Vyšehrad?

Even so, it's easy to imagine what a strong hold the Christian church once had at this old fortification. From its history of being the seat of Bohemian royalty and an army training center, all that's left are a huge church, a smaller church, and a Christian cemetery, along with a few mythical figures that were brought from somewhere else. Vyšehrad feels holy.

I walk out of the Leopold Gate, part of the Baroque fortifications. It's famous for being shown in the Miloš Forman film *Amadeus*, which shows the life of Wolfgang Amadeus Mozart from the point of view of a jealous rival.

I salute Forman for including a shot of this gate, presumably located in Vienna, during the bankrupt Mozart's ignoble burial in a commoner's grave in Vienna. Too bad poor old Mozart doesn't get a posthumous royalty from every Mozartkugel sold since his death.

Vyšehrad provides some of the most memorable views of Hradčany castle and is one of my [Jarda's] favorite green spaces in Prague. As you enter or exit, there are good restaurants for a quick snack or full meal, making Vyšehrad a popular site for Prague inhabitants and visitors alike.

AFTERWORD

During our travels to Prague from 1990 onward, we realized that we had become a part of the city, as Prague herself has folded us into her story. We were fortunate to meet in Prague people from all walks of life, of many nationalities, of diverse religious backgrounds, and from all kinds of professions.

When we lived in Prague, 2010-2013, we discovered that to live in Prague is to learn almost infinite patience; to love Prague is to accept imperfection as an integral part of beauty.

Perhaps the most important lesson Prague taught me, and has given to Sara and me, is the one I will carry as my life's motto: To live fully is to notice, to love, to care, and to see the small miracles that time hides in plain sight. To understand that endurance is not resistance and that grace is at least as important as seeing clearly; that love, like a city is built slowly—stone by stone, gesture by gesture, smile by smile—until it becomes something that outlasts us.

For Sara and me, now even “getting lost in Prague” is fun. Each corner reveals a new secret, a doorway carved with angels, a café filled with laughter, a fragment of music drifting from open windows. Like a bird awakening the others in one of Prague's many charming parks with a song, until all are singing a happy chorus, so just one positive thought about the city alerts and awakens others until the whole city is moving on a higher energy plane. Humor returns to our day, and joy steps in our "getting lost" experience in the ancient city, and we are found again.

If I learned anything from Prague by now, it is this: just as her streets and alleys are not straight or perfect but are meant to be walked, explored, and cherished, so the whole city is to be explored and cherished, each time we encounter it. And if at the end, someone remembers that we looked upon the world with wonder, that we listened, loved, prayed, and took time for quiet contemplation and laughter, then I think it's enough.

Thank you, Prague, for enhancing my enduring belief in the redemptive power of beauty, quiet contemplation, and the quiet strength of human endurance. Thank you for folding us into your story. Thank you for teaching us patience and giving us courage to persevere.

Jaroslav (Jarda) and Sara Tusek

FOR FURTHER READING: BOOKS ABOUT PRAGUE AND ITS SURROUNDINGS

Hugh Agnew, *The Czechs and the Lands of the Bohemian Crown*. Hoover Institution Press, 2013.

Mark Baker, *Lonely Planet Prague & Czechia* (Travel Guide). Lonely Planet, 2025.

Peter Demetz, *Prague in Black and Gold: Scenes in the Life of a European City*. Hill & Wang, New York, 1997.

Franz Kafka, *Metamorphosis* (1915). Various editions available.

Cynthia Paces, *Prague, the Heart of Europe*. Oxford University Press, 2025.

Prague: *A Traveler's Literary Companion*. Edited by Paul Wilson, Whereabouts Press, Berkeley, California, 1995.

Slavomir Ravik, *Praha známá – neznámá*. Levné knihy, 2005.

Jaroslav B. Tusek with Sara Tusek, *Leaders to Follow*. International Leadership Institute Publications, Lake Mary, FL, 2018.

Jaroslav B. and Sara D. Tusek, *Three Things You Can't Do in Prague*. Servant Leaders Press, 2006.

Sara Tusek, *Prague for Beginners: Finding Myself in Prague*. International Leadership Institute Publications, Lake Mary, FL, 2017.

Jaroslav Hašek, *The Good Soldier Schweik (Czech spelling Švejk),* first published in the 1920s. Newer editions published by Penguin Random House.

PRAGUE AND THE INTERNATIONAL LEADERSHIP INSTITUTE: A SOLID RELATIONSHIP SINCE 1990

Through our business, the International Leadership Institute (ILI), we [Jarda and Sara Tusek] have had a unique window into the transition of Prague from a sad, tired city neglected for forty years under communist rule to a vibrant, fast-changing city where the new and the old are harmoniously on display every day.

Our European and U.S.-based educational programs and services have brought us into contact with thousands of Prague business executives, academic leaders, ambitious students, government officials, and people from all walks of life who've shared with us what Prague is really all about.

Jarda founded ILI in Princeton, New Jersey in 1985 to provide international executive education programs for business leaders. So it was that when communism collapsed in Czechoslovakia in 1989, ILI was ready to bridge the gap between the old, state-planned economy and the new, globally-intertwined market. Sara was inspired by the dramatic events of the 1989 Velvet Revolution and became Jarda's partner in ILI.

Soon ILI found other partners (the Czech Ministry of Industry, Olomouc Training Center, the Jacksonville Chamber of Commerce, the University of North Florida, Jacksonville University, and the Slovak Chamber of Commerce and Industry, among others) to aid in delivering executive education programs to Czech and Slovak business leaders, bringing them to the U.S. for university classes and business internships to jump-start their company's entry into the international market.

ILI programs have brought hundreds of Czech and Slovak participants to the U.S. for the period of three months, and later, also participants from Lithuania, Macedonia, Croatia, Bulgaria, Romania, and Ukraine for shorter, custom-tailored U.S. Aid programs in cooperation with the U.S. Department of State, Agency for International Development.

At the same time, ILI has been leading tours of Prague for Americans and visitors from all over the world from 1990 through 2013, introducing them to a country that had been hidden for four decades. And in the summer months, we've hosted European students in our American English Language Immersion programs, giving the students a chance to learn American English with a host family and in university classes.

We've distilled all of these experiences in Prague into this little guide. Our many returns to Prague for business and personal reasons have given us a perspective, over thirty-six years, of the ongoing changes and the colorful history of the city.

Without the city of Prague, we would have had no exciting programs, no eager executive participants, no inquiring students, and no way to get an insider's view of modern Prague. And so we say, "thank you, Prague" for your many generous gifts to us and your kind forbearance of our efforts to make a positive impact on the people in the energetic city of Prague.

www.ingramcontent.com/pod-product-compliance
Lightning Source LLC
LaVergne TN
LVHW010703110826
845149LV00014B/3205

* 9 7 9 8 9 9 5 7 2 5 6 0 2 *